CALM COLOURING
MINDFULNESS

100 CREATIVE DESIGNS TO COLOUR IN

Relax and unwind with this stress-relieving colouring book of meditative artworks. The art of colouring is a relaxing activity, focusing the mind and stilling the endless mental chatter that saps our energy and causes stress. As you start to colour in these beautiful designs you will unleash your inner creativity and find yourself gradually moving to a more peaceful and calming state of mind.

You can colour in as little or as much as you like, taking your time to develop your picture the way you want it. There are no hard and fast rules, you are truly free to create your own unique designs whether you choose pencils, pens or paints. Start colouring today and enjoy the still, quiet voice of calm this soothing practice will bring you.

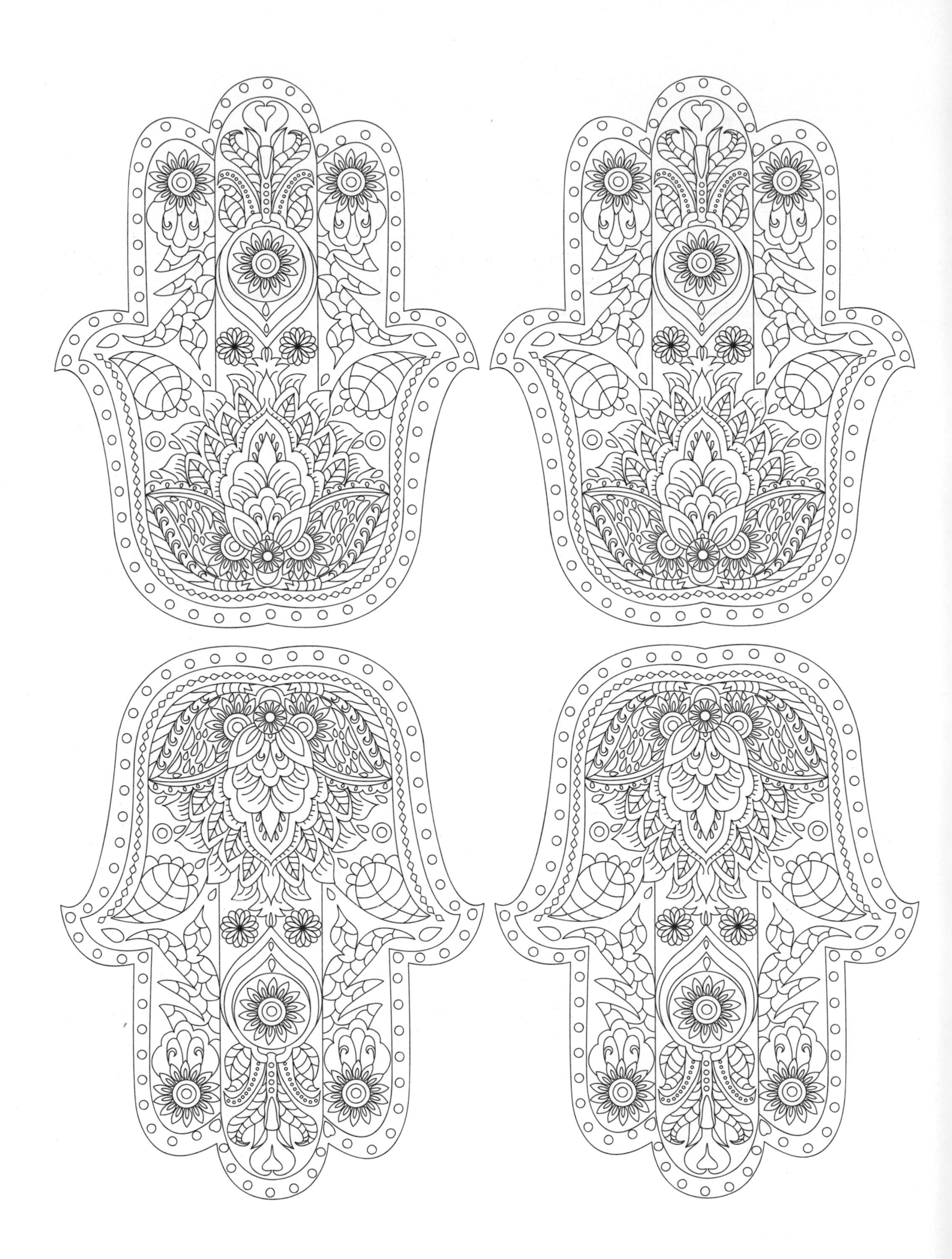

This edition is published by Southwater
an imprint of Anness Publishing Ltd,
108 Great Russell Street, London WC1B 3NA;
info@anness.com

www.lorenzbooks.com; www.annesspublishing.com;
twitter: @Anness_Books

Images courtesy of Shutterstock